# Attract Women

## How to Seduce Your Dream Girl(s) with Body Language and Put Her(Them) to Bed

### VICTORIA LYNX

# Copyright

## ATTRACT WOMEN

## HOW TO SEDUCE YOUR DREAM GIRL(S) WITH BODY LANGUAGE AND PUT HER(THEM) TO BED

*Copyright © Blue Labyrinth Pte Ltd, 2019*

The transmission, duplication or reproduction of any of the following work including specific information will be considered an illegal act irrespective of if it is done electronically or in print. This extends to creating a secondary or tertiary copy of the work or a recorded copy and is only allowed with express written consent from the Publisher. All additional right reserved.

The information in the following pages is broadly considered to be a truthful and accurate account of facts and as such any inattention, use or misuse of the information in question by the reader will render any resulting actions solely under their purview. There are no scenarios in which the publisher or the original author of this work can be in any fashion deemed liable for any hardship or damages that may befall them after undertaking information described herein.

Additionally, the information in the following pages is intended only for informational purposes and should thus be thought of as universal. As befitting its nature, it is presented without assurance regarding its prolonged validity or interim quality. Trademarks that are mentioned are done without written consent and can in no way be considered an endorsement from the trademark holder.

*Copyright © Blue Labyrinth Pte Ltd, 2019*

# Table of Contents

# Foreword

Thank you, and thank you again for purchasing your very own copy of *Attract Women*. I promise this will be just the beginning for your upcoming, exciting journey!

Did you know that around 90 percent of all communication occurs non-verbally and the fairer sex is extremely good at picking and reading body language signals you're giving? It is a big YES, and it seems more like a scary prospect. However, use it right, and you can brilliantly turn this into an alpha male SUPER-POWER.

Experts have stated that even when you are dating, the verbal language is often relegated to subordinate status. It's the non-verbal communication or body language that gains prominence. Women are instinctive creatures (or monsters), who have more awareness on non-verbal communication related to body language. They are SUPER efficient when it comes to deciphering non-verbal cues, even if you are stating just the opposite of it verbally. Scary again? You bet!

This means if you are saying you are totally into someone, but your body language reveals. Otherwise, women are not likely to believe what you say!

# Chapter 1

# It Does NOT Matter Even If You Are the Ugliest Dude on Earth

Ever realized why sometimes even the most average looking men are natural chick magnets, who have women flocking to them like moths. There's got to be something that they are doing right. They are just ordinary guys with extraordinary body language skills. Their top-notch body language creates a hypnotic, magnetic charm that attracts women by the dozen.

What are these powerful body language secrets that are the key to winning a woman's heart and getting her in bed? Is it only confidence, independence, charisma or another collection of "x" factors or mojo?

I'll let you in on a little secret that can be used to your advantage. Most men possess a body language that screams "I am absolutely used to the idea of being liked and received by the opposite sex. Run miles away from me."

The reality is that owning an appealing body language will make you stand out from the average Joes struggling with their non-verbal communication. Truth be told —a majority of men give out terrible, desperate and unattractive non-verbal clues. There, you've spotted a loophole already and can gain an edge by learning the finer nuances of impressing your dream woman with seductive body language.

Do you know the number one reason why men fail to build a dating and sex life of their dreams? They just don't have a clue about how to take actions and charm women they desire. They are unable to overpower their compelling fear of rejection. They weigh themselves under the weight of how to be good enough for the woman. Men want to kiss, seduce, capitulate with women, without having a clue about how to be a man a woman just can't resist.

In reality, seduction is an art and science. They are several subtle body languages and scientific mind tricks that can be used to make yourself absolutely irresistible to women. From persuasion through gestures and expressions to voice and tone cues, this book has plenty of little-known strategies and secret tips that will put you on the highway to being the ultimate alpha male. There are plenty of psychological techniques that can be used to attract desirable women if you know how to play them in the right way.

Alpha males use unbelievably stealthy seduction tricks that help them make really bold and fast moves. One minute you'll spot him talking to a woman, the next moment they will get into a cab heading to her home. The man's actions are appealing simply because he is aware of how to behave around attractive women. These men know exactly how to display the perfect body language, listen to women, how to touch women in the right way, and build just the right measure of sexual tension.

To enhance your individual body language, you must work towards making it what you want, and then imbibe it as an almost subconscious part of your personality. It will be one of the things that come most naturally to you when you present yourself in front of women.

Body language plays on a very scientific and subconscious level. When your body language is positive and confident, the subconscious mind receives signals of being confident, self-assured, and in control.

It quickly recognizes these body language clues as a sign of unwavering confidence, and later directs the body (gestures, posture, expressions, movement) to behave in a more confident and self-assured manner. Thus, it is a cycle, the subconscious mind is led to believe that you are a confident person, which it reinforces through non-verbal signals that reveal even more confident, in control behavior.

Include the examples, secret strategies and subtle seduction techniques discussed in the book to send the right non-verbal signals to women. Of course, you won't go from being a struggling Joe to the ultimate alpha male in a day. However, with time, impressing women will become a second skin.

Fasten your seatbelts and get ready for an enjoyable adventure that trains you to pick-up the ultimate body language tricks to woo your dream woman.

# Chapter 2

# You Have Only FOUR Seconds to Impress Her

Did you know people meeting you for the first time form an impression about you in the initial four seconds? Hard truth? You bet!  If you want to go from being a weekend Netflix binge-watcher to a guy who is never short of dates, you got to be a dude who creates a stellar first impression. If there's one secret sauce or magic potion when it comes to wooing a woman, it's creating a powerful initial impression.

Deep research into the science of seduction reveals that attraction isn't confined to a single domain. It is a combination of neurology (NLP), psychology, sexual studies, and evolutionary science, which is why I am revealing the ten most super awesome tips when it comes to sweeping a woman off her feet in the first meeting.

## Maintain a Relaxed Posture

Get this straight and clear, women absolutely don't dig men who go all nervous and jittery at the idea of introducing themselves to women. Nervousness is the biggest first impression killer.

Stay calm, relaxed and in control to create a magnificent first impression. Make sure the smallest gestures (often subconscious) such as holding your glass (hold it sideways and not in front) and standing (leaning against a wall is incredibly sexy) appear relaxed.

Leaning back will up your game like no other. When you are in a sitting or standing pose, simply lean back and look relaxed. This open and inviting gesture demonstrates that you're warm and approachable. Added tip – Let your arms loose by the side. Avoid leaning forward and crossing your arms. It shows a more closed, protected and shielded approach, where you are not open to being approached by strangers. Play smooth by sitting back in a relaxed posture, and you'll appear totally in control and approachable.

It indicates to the woman that you aren't trying too hard to impress, and you are an extremely confident and self-assured individual. To women, it isn't a huge deal to approach them and talk to them. If you get rattled about something as non-fuss (in their eyes) as this, it indicates that you are incapable of handling bigger challenges.

I'll let you in on a cool secret. I know most men are a bundle of nerves in front of women they fancy. To keep yourself calm, relaxed (and almost Zen-like), practice taking slow, relaxed breaths focused on the belly. Witness your stomach rising and falling as you take well-defined, slow and deep breaths. Don't take tensed, rushed breaths into the lungs. This tightens your muscles and makes your overall body language appear tensed and nervous.

Give your muscles an opportunity to relax. Once the stress and tension alleviate, it is easier to radiate natural confidence. Your body will be shining with a fresh lease of confidence, and women will invariably be attracted to you.

Do not slump over or slouch while approaching a woman or introducing yourself to someone for the first time. She'll be scooting in another direction before you finish saying hello. Slumping, crossing arms and looking at the floor will kill your chances of creating a positive first impression. It isn't a very appealing stance, especially when you're meeting someone for the first time, and reflects low confidence and a more negative attitude.

Always hold yourself high physically and mentally. Pull back your shoulders and keep your head straight up. Act like you're a man who deserves a woman's affection, admiration, and attention. Women (or for that matter) find people who know their true worth absolutely irresistible.

Women feel more at ease in the company of men who are relaxed, self-assured, and confident about themselves.

## Avoid Acting Distracted

Women don't take it kindly if they are relegated to secondary status. If you fancy them, they should be the center of your attention. Don't move around or act fidgety around a woman you desire. Preoccupation and distraction are huge turn-offs. You're not giving off a very flattering vibe to the object of your desire if you make perpetually fidgeting and nervous gestures. A man who is in control of his body language will be taken more seriously than one who is awkward with his gestures and movements. Keep your feet slightly apart while sitting, which will prevent you from constantly shifting your weight from one side to another.

Shifty, fidgety and distracted gestures are a huge sign of nervousness that takes away from an essentially calm, confident and relaxed demeanor, which you want to portray.

Don't make too many confusing gestures that send the woman you desire perplexing non-verbal signals. Twitching your body excessively or making too many animated hand gestures is an absolute no-no. It gives off the feeling that you aren't very comfortable with your body and leaves a damp first impression. When you appear uncomfortable with your own body, how to you expect women to be comfortable near you?

Of course, you don't have to be all over the woman and shower her with unwanted attention. That's a huge no-no too. Acting a little indifferent to things happening around you is all right; just don't act too fidgety and distracted. Cool indifference is mighty appealing; nervousness is not.

A majority of men falter here. They believe it's cool to act all busy and distracted to impress a woman. So, what does Mr. X do? Whip out a smartphone from his pocket and pretend to be occupied with important matters. What does it reveal to the lady? You're simply not interested enough to give her undivided attention. Well, don't blame her for getting the impression that you want to be somewhere else.

Instead of appearing distracted, keep all objects of distraction away and appear interested in your immediate surroundings. Keep your body language alert, focused and aware of your environment. Put your head up, and relish the moment, which makes you appear more approachable. Plus, you pick up all the silent, non-verbal invitations/signals women stealthily send you.

If you really want to score with a woman, avoid showing too much emotion or reaction to things happening around you in the first meeting. Display a more unaffected demeanor. Let others play the guessing game about how you think and feel. This makes the challenge of getting to know you up, close and personal even more compelling.

Stay at the top of your dating/seduction game by showing you are always in control and relaxed. Everyone loves people who own the situation.

## Grab Your Space You Star

Guess what? Even though we have evolved from our primitive existence, our subconscious mind is still deeply hard-wired in its patterns when it comes to relationships and social gestures. There's a reason we still mark our territory physically and subconsciously, and entering our space leads us to act in a more territorial manner.

Well okay, no one's asking you to grab the limelight by acting weird or hyper-energetic. One way to demonstrate confidence when meeting a woman you desire for the first time is to take your own space. Don't be the nerd who fades into the background, while others hog center stage.

You don't want to stand out for the wrong reason, but that doesn't mean you don't get noticed (which is equally bad if you ask me). Own your zone and take up your space immediately. Expert tip for owning your space – seize up the space within 3 feet as your own private space. Think of yourself as owning that private bubble and ensuring any woman who passes through it has a great time. Focus on completely owning the space around you, and you'll have the gathering's hottest gals noticing you.

Somebody language and seduction experts suggest taking as much space as you can. If you are seated in the lobby, lean behind and spread out your legs. This is a subconscious, territorial instinct that women notice. Well, in the woman's mind, if you are occupying a lot of "territory," you are the room's alpha male. The one who is in command, as well as fun, confident and laid-back.

## A Sexy Voice Wins the Day (And Night)

Ever wondered why women are attracted like moths to a fireball by men with deep, husky and low-pitched voices? Women are essentially auditory creatures who are instantly attracted to a calm, strong, and controlled voice or tone.

Talk too fast, and you'll come across as nervous. Speak slowly, and you'll run the risk of appearing dumb. Keep your tone steady, unwavering and well-paced. Make a conscious effort to make yourself audience and clear by speaking slower than you usually do while talking to a woman. It will award you greater control of what you're saying (plus you'll time to think about what you're going to say next).

Avoid stressing about mistakes and stammering during the conversation. Even if you do make a mistake while speaking, cover it up by saying something humorous quickly to salvage the situation. Think and speak according to the situation.

Something like, "Ah! Damn, this is exactly what happens when you're in the company of sweepingly attractive women. You totally forget what you want to say." This will not just be flattering to the lady but also make you come across as high on wit and humor. Self-deprecating humor is a sign of huge confidence.

Sometimes while talking, pause for a moment and appear serious. This creates an aura of power, influencer and confidence.

## Open Up Dude

You don't want the woman of your dreams to think you're a closed, secretive and guarded person. Of course, you don't want to come across as a sparrow on steroids but keeping an open and approachable demeanor works to create a glowing first impression.  I'll let you in on all secret body language strategies to appear warm, open and approachable. To begin with, keep your palms facing upwards (open and exposed). Remember, how you reveal all your cards by flashing your palms upwards in a game? Well, you aren't exactly revealing all your cards here. However, you are demonstrating a more "open to you baby" kind of demeanor.

Another big cross on the list of things to avoid is crossing your legs or arms while standing or sitting. Even if you don't realize, it has "closed" written on it in bold. You are psychologically blocking yourself from your wonder woman. Another vehement no-no, if you're holding a drink, don't hold it right in front of you. Hold the glass down, sideways.

Master these little-known techniques that most men don't have a clue about to enjoy an edge over them when it comes to garnering attention from the opposite sex.

Hide your feelings by all means but keep the hands open. Also, displaying a lightly off the limits or playing hard to get body language doesn't hurt. You need to keep a fine balance between not acting too distant (will make it appear you aren't interested) and not acting too eager (which makes you come across as desperate).

According to research conducted by Timothy Wilson and Erin Whitchurch of the University of Virginia, acting slightly indifferent towards women can lead them to contemplate your distant behavior, and eventually, develop a liking for you.

## Be the Leader of Your Pack

This again dates back to our evolutionary genes. Women are innately attracted to powerful men or leaders who are in control of their pack. Going back to primitive times, men who were powerful group leaders were seen as highly desirable sexual mates in the mating game. This hasn't changed much since are genetics remain the same.

Women are deeply attracted to men in position and authority at a very subconscious level. So how do you be the man who is in charge of people around him? You can very well demonstrate this from across the table or room.

A simple tip for revealing your leadership prowess is to touch people you are conversing with. Pat men on the back encouragingly. Place your hand on people's shoulders within a brief moment. Do a high five or punch someone playfully.

Well, research in a publication called *Why Women Have Sex* suggests that women often see men who touch people surrounding them as possessing brilliant leadership skills. They view these men as someone is a position of authority, influence, inspiration, and power. According to women, these are the guys who earn respect. So something as effortless as making slight physical contact with people around you shows you in a flattering, commanding light.

Psychologically, women have an intrinsic sense of identifying leaders within a group. Men who look authoritative and confident are naturally attractive when it comes to seducing a woman. To work this perfect leader strategy, you have to smile, stand, sit and walk like you don't care about what everyone thinks.

Work on your alpha male strategy before pulling this off at the next party or gathering. Make yourself look valuable by enhancing your physical looks, leadership skills, and charisma. This will make women yearn for your attention instead of the other way.

Avoid putting anyone, especially the woman you fancy on a subconscious pedestal. You can permanently bid adieu to all your chances of dating and seducing the woman once you place her on a high pedestal. If you are overtly revealing how much you're drooling over her, you are just giving her a secret, unspoken power to dump you whenever she wants.

It is easy for you to lose the woman's respect, affection and subconscious power once you elevate them to a higher pedestal. Make the woman feel that you are too good for her, and she has to make a real effort to get someone as valuable as you.

## Be Positive, or at least Try to Act Positive

Well, it's not just a blood group but a way of life that'll make you compulsively attractive to women. If you are in a positive frame of mind (operating with positive thoughts and a feel-good attitude), it'll not miss showing in your body language effortlessly.

You will invariably come across as more friendly, warm, approachable and relaxed. Can I give you a brilliant technique for maintaining a positive attitude? Have a happy go-to song that you hum to yourself each time you want to feel positive and peppy. This tune should transform you into a happy, feel-good zone while elevating your energy level and mood. Another effective way?

Take some time to focus on aspects you appreciate in others and yourself. This gives your steps added bounce, and it doesn't go unnoticed by women. It leaves women wondering what makes you so upbeat, and hey presto before you even say "positive," they've clamored to you to get their share of that radiant, infectious positive energy.

## Walk the Talk

Well, what's that we've heard about don't walk like you own the world, walk like you don't care who does! Walk with your head held down, and you've ruined it even before beginning.

When you walk in with your hands tucked inside the pocket, man do you look completely off limits or unapproachable. Leave your hands dangling sideways, keep your back erect and tilt your head slightly. Next, stick out your chest, and draw your shoulders firmly back.  This again reveals a natural confidence.

Have you ever observed a millionaire or celebrity? They are almost always walking exactly as described above, radiating confidence that's hard to ignore. There's a powerful and commanding aura each time they enter a room. That is the kind of arresting attention you want to attract from women.

A man's walking style since primitive times is subconsciously viewed as him approaching a woman for the purpose of mating. Taking firm, confident and well-paced strides is a sign of someone who knows what he wants and how to get it.

Take, for instance, you're in a store and fancy a girl. What is the best way to approach her? Walk confidently towards her with two shirts, trousers or any piece of clothing really (just leave out the intimate wear for now though). Don't stammer or appear nervous. Simply ask her which of the two pieces does she thinks is better.

Well, depending on how smooth your conversation skills are (can be developed like everything else), converse with her for a minute. If all goes well, and you've charmed her enough, go for the kill and ask for her number. Rocket science? No!

## Subtle Bragging

Well, you don't want to give your dream woman the impression that the entire universe revolves around you by talking only about your accomplishments. However, you have to speak about the good things too. Otherwise, how are you going to create a favorable and irresistible impression?

The best strategy to get a woman to fall head over heels in love with you is to very briefly and subtly mention your achievements or attributes. Don't linger or dwell on them for too long like it's a huge deal for you. Pretend that these are regular everyday things for you. Another important thing to consider is that you don't belittle her accomplishments to make yours look really big.

For instance, if you have to attend an awards ceremony to collect an award for excellent workplace performance, drop a subtle hint about how you will be busy on the day of the ceremony under some pretext. Similarly, if you are buying a new car or house, mention briefly about how you're busy looking at new homes and cars. Just mention your achievements or acquisitions lightly without focusing on them.

## Build an Emotional Rapport

The journey from meeting a woman to taking her to bed becomes surprisingly easy when you build a powerful emotional rapport with her. Psychologically, mirroring is one of the most effective ways to forge a strong mental connection with the woman you desire. Start mirroring the way she stands, speaks, holds her glass and gesticulates.

Keep it discreet and don't make it look like you are aping her. Subconsciously, mirroring sends the other person a message that you are pretty much like them and makes it easier for them to connect with you on a mental plane. Gradually mimic her posture or use the same words/phrases as she does. Once you practice this strategy, it will come effortlessly.

For example, if the woman holds her glass on her left side, try and hold your glass of drink on the left side too. If they are making a particular gesture with their hands, try and make that gesture too for conveying that you identify with what they are trying to communicate, and acknowledging the same.

Mirroring works wonderfully well because it is seen as something that's beyond the realm of our conscious awareness. When you repeat someone's actions and words, you are secretly sending signals of familiarity to them through the subconscious.

Seduction boy language experts suggest that you should mirror or mimic a specific gesture three seconds after it is first noticed. This lets you imitate a person without them freaking out or becoming suspicious about your behavior. Although on the face of it, you are simply mirroring the lady's body language, the end goal is to match her feelings, views, thoughts and yes – maybe even the breathing pattern. Even minor actions like posture, expressions, blinking, verbal acknowledgments, and scratching should be matched. If this technique is implemented correctly, the woman will be falling like you like a pack of cards!

Another quick way to build an emotional rapport is to reveal a vulnerability in the correct manner. According to research, some women are taken in by weaker men. However, weakness is also a relative trait. Remember to never make the blunder of revealing low value and terrible weaknesses. This may really go against you. For example, you may want to narrate a sob story related to your ex, but this will only make you look like a crybaby who cannot move on.

If you are using this psychological trick, ensure you pick your weaknesses with care and don't opt for weaknesses that make you look low-value or unflattering. Instead of concentrating on your past, build emotional rapport via future projections. How about an exciting thing you've fantasizing about all along? Talk about an exciting travel experience that's on the top of your bucket list. Just reveal some fun things without overdoing it. You are doing nothing but controlling the woman's mind without making her realize.

Women possess way more powerful and vivid imagination than men, which makes them see the exciting things in her mind's eye. Also, you've shared a personal dream or goal with her, which makes you instantly adorable to her. Practice this technique regularly and keep watching for the body language of couples who are already in the rapport building stage. You'll witness amazing results in little time.

# Chapter 3

# Mind Control is No Longer a Dream

If you want to seduce a woman and get her to bed, you have to be able to control her mind and emotions, while making her feel comfortable. Making her yearn for spending more time with your needs more than just regular pampering or opening doors for her. It is about connecting with her at a subconscious level by applying a host of psychological strategies.

Psychological strategies, manipulations, and persuasion doesn't always imply sneaky tricks to lure and emotionally destroy women for your own benefit. If used positively, it can be used for helping you both get into a mutually fulfilling and gratifying relationship. Here are 10 little-known yet brilliantly effective strategies when it comes to controlling a woman's mind and emotions.

## Eye Contact

Maintaining consistent and unwavering direct eye contact is the key to displaying your interest in a woman. It not just depicts supreme confidence but also reinforces your intention to seduce the other person, thus establishing a ground for taking the woman you desire to bed. Holding continuous eye contact during a conversation is a psychological sign of attraction. It also works on a physiological level.

When we establish eye contact with someone, we really fancy, our pupils start dilating. Even if a person doesn't instantly notice your dilating pupils, at a subconscious level, they catch the signal. This only attracts the person further to us. Keep in mind that you don't overdo it or the other person will start feeling uncomfortable or freaked out.

Whatever happens, avoid looking down every now and then. Nothing is unsexier than a guy who keeps shifting his glance to the floor. It makes things come across as awkward and uncomfortable.

Research has proven that looking down constantly can have a negative impact on your and the other person's mental state. Keep things positive by fixating your gaze on the woman you desire. She'll be flattered and reward you with equal attention.

Making continuous eye contact can be a great seduction tool, more so if you can add a seductive smirk and raise your eyebrows a bit while doing it. Mighty irresistible? You bet.

## Touching for Establishing Attraction

If you don't want to get friendzoned dear friend, by all means, work hard towards developing some kind of sexual tension with the woman you've just started dating. Cruel as it sounds, women often make up their mind within a couple of dates (most of the time it's just one) about guys they want to friend zone and those they are sexually attracted to.

You need to work with touches just right to build the perfect sexual chemistry or risk blowing it up. It shouldn't come across as desperate or negative, all the same, you don't have to be a limp player who is afraid to make a move when it comes to revealing his fondness for a woman. Don't start grabbing a woman too early on in the dating period.

Stick to light touching during the first couple of dates. Begin with hugs, brushing lightly against her arms and leaning or sitting close to her. Lightly brush your arms against hers and let go immediately. Tap her hands or palms lightly and again let go. Don't linger the touch for long. It should be brief enough for her to crave more of it.

You'll quickly gather how comfortable a woman is with your touch by reading her non-verbal signals. If she pulls off or backs off instinctively, she may not be very open to the idea of touching at this stage in the relationship. However, if she smiles, appears relaxed and seems to be having a good time, that's a definite signal she digs your actions.

There's no common yardstick for what you can or can't-do in the touch department during the initial few dates. You have to be perceptive enough to understand what the woman desires and make your moves accordingly. Slow, smooth movements are appreciated by women. Don't rush things or be rough with a woman. Chances are you'll never see again in your life.

Breaking the physical touch hindrance isn't a big deal if you do it right. Once you've spent many hours together as friends or dating partners, there's a comfort level that makes it easy for the woman to relate to you.

Start gently by offering a goodbye hug that doesn't linger for more than a few seconds (3-5 seconds). Judge her reaction to knowing how comfortable the woman is. If she squeezes back tightly or holds you for long, she may just be ready to move to the next level. Similarly, reach out to her hand and brush against it gently. If she grabs your hand tightly or quickly intertwines her pretty fingers in yours, the woman is into you.

Each time you're parting ways tell her something like, "Alright sweets, I feel like a good bear hug today. Give me a nice goodbye hug and then gently proceed to hug her for a couple of seconds. Make it warm and affectionate, and not like all you want to do is feel her breasts or brush your hardness against her. Give her a few seconds to enjoy the feeling, but make it brief enough for her to yearn for it in future.

Flash her your most dazzling smile after the hug and confidently in a way that's unique to you, "hey, do you realize how beautiful/gorgeous you are (avoid saying seductive, sexy, hot, etc. unless you've reached that comfort level with her)" Add I really dig/like you in the end. This tells her you're after more, and interested in taking it to the next level.

It is easy to break a woman's unspoken touch barrier if you know how to be charmingly flirtatious. Hold a lady's hand and lead her to the bar. Place your arm lightly on her lower back. The idea is to get her comfortable to your touch.

## Capture the Lady's Senses

Well, much as you're in denial about this, physical attractiveness goes a long way for getting a woman to go to bed with you. Make it a sensory bonanza for her by increasing your attractiveness quotient. Wear comfortable and well-fitting attire in a color that flatters you. Sport a haircut that looks chic, well-groomed and suits your face cut. Smell good, as you're going to be remembered by your smell. Don't make it a very overpowering scent. Keep it nice and subtle, yet compellingly fragrant.

Research has consistently pointed out that the most critical factor when it comes to awakening a person's sexual desires is the smell. This is because pheromones are responsible for triggering sexual desires. Once you can influence her sensory experiences, it is easy to charm her.

A study conducted by the University of Management in Singapore revealed that women are highly attracted to men with broad faces since it demonstrates a powerful and masculine persona. I know what you're smirking and saying there, how can I change the shape of my face dude? Nope, you can and don't have to alter the shape of your face. However, you can use tricks to make your face look broader. For instance, you may want to grow a beard or develop some facial muscles by working out in the gym. Women love strong and powerful men, and some physical features convey just that.

Physical attractiveness attributes play on a very subconscious level to attract women. They facilitate or support your body language or non-verbal attraction clues to make you appear insanely irresistible to women.

## Smile

A smile conveys affiliation, relation, and affection. It is a sign of taking to someone instantly or being attracted to a person. Flashing a genuine smile communicates confidence, positivity, and lovingness in the mind of the person you're out with. Don't expect a woman to jump straight into bed with you as soon as you flash your pearls.

However, it will set the tone for a friendly and affectionate relationship that can lead to bigger things. Once you've established a warm relationship rapport, it is easy to move to more intimate and advanced touch strategies.

Psychologically, you're showing your interest or affection for the woman.

## Use Your Ears

Much as many mistaken dudes like to believe, impressing a woman isn't about talking nineteen to the dozen until she needs a pill to cure her headache. It is as much about listening attentively to a person to win her affection.

Unlike men, who are more to the point, women love to have extended and long-drawn conversations. They are high on details and the backdrop of every subject/topic they are discussing. If you want to charm your lady, listen keenly to everything she's saying. Offer small acknowledgments that you are listening to her intently.

 It can be anything from a nod to a simple yes to exclamations – whatever suits the situation and communicates to her that you are listening to her or completely immersed in the conversation.

One of the most important things when it comes to listening to a woman is to hold back your advice and suggestions. Bite your tongue if you have to but don't offer suggestions or solutions. Much as you want to make her life simpler, simply hold back from giving any advice unless asked for.

Men often share their problems to get solutions, whereas women share their problems simply to talk it out with someone who understands. They are not necessarily looking for guidance or expert advice or someone who treats them like they know nothing. Hence resist the urge to play agony uncle and just listen to her.

Empathize with her, show understanding/concern and just let her know you're there if she needs anything. Don't offer her a 10-point strategy to combat the problem, because you'll end up creating a new problem for yourself.

Listen with interest to stories about her buddies or something she found funny. You don't have to be a yes man and agree with everything. Put your point across in a gentle and non-offensive manner. At times, repeat what she's just said to let her know that you are actively listening.

Avoid talking excessively about yourself. It's alright to give a brief introduction about your background, education, career, hobbies etc. However, don't go overboard with details about yourself. Again, keep your eyes glued to her. Avoid looking at other women or talking too much about them. Ensure you focus on the woman you're with and make her feel special. You need to give her impression that she's the only one who matters. And for god's sake, put that phone away when she's talking.

## She's Always Testing You

There's no escaping the fact that women are almost always testing men. She's almost always looking for different ways to understand what's going in your mind or your intentions. For instance, if a woman is deeply attracted to you, she may pretend that she doesn't really dig you just to see your reaction/response.

What she wants to establish is that you are a confident and self-assured individual who isn't afraid to hold himself even in the face of rejection. This makes you a highly appealing man in her eyes. Don't get bogged down by her lack of attention or indifference to you. Hold your position throughout your interaction without appearing fazed.

It's a very primordial, instinctive and evolutionary thing for women. If your confidence crumbles or shakes, the woman doesn't view you as being worthy of a male or holding a masculine position. It is easier for her to play the role of the protected. Well, what do they say about making her feel like a real lady? It simply allows women to be more feminine around a man who is powerful. When a woman feels innately feminine in your presence, she will inevitably be turned on by your masculinity.

Ensure that you come across as confident and not egomaniacal. There is a thin line yet huge difference between the two, especially when it comes to presenting yourself to others. Confidence is deeply rooted in being comfortable in your own skin, and with what you are doing. An ego-driven 0r egomaniacal personality, on the other hand, fundamentally stems from insecurity or negative self-emotions. Bragging is a huge no-no when it comes to seducing or attracting a woman.

Keep things cool and subtle. Humility makes you sexier. Remember, guys who are innately comfortable in their skin are more likely to impress women than show-offs who operate from the point of jealousy or insecurity. Well, six-pack abs will help your cause, but they aren't a necessity.

## Identify Common Ground

One of the best strategies for getting a woman to like you or feel a sense of belongingness/affiliation for you is to identify a common ground. Talk about something you both have in common to create a comfort level that can take things to another level. It can be anything from shared moments to hobbies to favorite sports teams to political affiliations. Establishing a common ground makes it easier for you to seduce a woman.

If you gather early in the conversation that a particular topic completely lights up her face, keep dropping it into the conversation every now and then.

Appealing to a lady's sense of humor is almost always the best way to get her to sleep with you. It will invariably up your chances of getting the woman you desire to hop into bed with you. Ever wondered why the nearly scary looking Russell Brand had earned so much success in bed? Just Ensure the lady is laughing with you and not at how ridiculous you are.

Clowns aren't a turn on for women. However, men are comfortable and confident enough to display a clever sense of humor are insanely appealing. Even when you are humorous, don't try too hard to recite lines from the latest best-selling pick-up manual. Make it sound natural and unforced. It should come across as intrinsic to your personality and not something that requires too much effort.

Put the woman at ease by treading in the domain of subjects she appears to be comfortable with. Making a woman feel relaxed, positive and comfortable is the key to get her to open up and talk about more intimate things. Get her to laugh or keep her glued to the conversation by asking a couple of interesting questions that get her talking.

Make it a mix of spontaneity and planned questions to avoid conversation lulls and awkward moments. The best advice when it comes to impressing a woman is to try to be yourself unless you're an absolute idiot. Then try to be less of an idiot.

## Enter the Woman's Comfort Zone

When you're alone with the woman, sit physically close to her. Act like you really didn't notice your physical proximity. If you've only been flirting with her, this is the time to get physically and subconsciously close to her. You are symbolically and literally entering her personal space to build a kind of sexual chemistry.

If she's simply seeing you as someone to flirt with, you need to show her you mean business. Don't make her feel uncomfortable by plonking yourself a little short of her lap. That's not the point. The idea is to show her that you are sexually interested in her AND want to take things to the next level.

Once you enter her space, try to make an attempt to lightly touch her arms or fingers. Keep your hand lovingly over hers. Slowly wrap your hand around her waist to create a feeling of belongingness and intimacy.

Psychologically, you are entering her space and making her feel comfortable with the idea of sharing her space with you.

One surefire way to winning a woman's affection (and eventually landing her in bed), is to build an intense rapport with her. Begin by making her feel easy in your presence by picking subjects that you know she is familiar with. Once you've grabbed her attention, and have her hooked, tease her lightly and appear playful. Ensure you keep it harmless and don't reveal right up that you are attracted to her. The strategy is to simply draw her closer and later quickly move away to leave her gasping for breath. It's the same scientific, magnetic principle, where there's plenty of attraction when unlike poles meet.

## Use Fractionation

This is another effective psychological technique used by seduction ninjas. It claims to make women fall for you in as little as 15 minutes or less. The technique is deeply embedded in hypnosis, with inspiration from the theories of both Sigmund Freud and Carl Jung.

The psychological technique involves taking women through an intensely emotional roller coaster to build a strong rapport. Fractionation is known for equipping men with plenty of seduction powers, which helps them enjoy a lot of success with the fairer sex.

Though known to be a highly effective seduction technique, fractionation is looked down upon many as being manipulative and unfair to the woman. It is controversial for being an amoral, dark and unethical seduction technique, similar to brains-washing. It's more like a dark hack and should be applied with discretion.

If you really want to understand fractionation, look at any of the soap operas. They take the viewer through an emotional roller coaster ride with a steady stream of suddenly positive and negative emotions. The audience thus becomes heavily invested in these heart-wrenching emotional sagas. Now you know why women love soap operas!

Fractionation is a mind control technique that involves a combination of voice, hypnosis, words and body language to elicit a strong emotional reaction from a woman to persuade her to get into bed with you.

It begins by building an emotional bond by getting her to trust you and open up to you. Ask lots of questions that demonstrate you are one of her leagues. Later, weave a powerful conversation that triggers strong emotional ups and downs. It can be as simple as initially asking her to describe something that makes her genuinely happy, and later, the saddest moment of her life or something that she deeply fears. Repeat the same sequence, and she'll be smitten.

When women experience positive and negative emotions in a short span, they are sold. Add your own unique aura (conversation skills, personality, body language), and she'll be melting in your arms. This isn't rocket science but a simple psychological premise.

When an individual (especially women since they are intrinsically emotional) is subjected to polarity (the brain is subjected to a series of feelings such as pleasure followed by pain followed by another sequence of pleasure and pain), it leads to a powerful emotional rapport. You're mentally enslaving her. However, caution against using this technique negatively. It may end up creating a lot of trouble in your and the woman's life.

Here are some instances of creating polarity.

"It feels so wonderful to have your best friend by your side through the ups and downs of life, right? I had the best buddy anyone could ask for. One fine day she just became sick and passed away all of a sudden. She was simply gone, without any warning.

Have you fallen in love with a person almost immediately and felt a deep connection? Like you know you just know from within that it's meant to be forever. I lived through that feeling once. We grew close so quickly. Only a few weeks after we got together, Faye died in a car crash. I mean she just left me and went."

See what I've done there? Built a soap opera like emotional graph to take your woman through a clear high (happiness), followed by an equally compelling low (sorrow). This helps her experience a deep psychological bonding with you.

If used right, this method can bring a woman in your control in no time. Fractionation is potentially more effective than the "secret seduction sauce" used by sneaky pickup artists. Bear in mind one hazard – it is impossible to undo the effects of this technique once it is applied. Once a woman has been psychologically enslaved with this method, leaving her like a hot potato will cause her immense psychological damage.

Therefore, tread with extreme caution and use this strategy ethically, positively and responsibly. You want to impress women not scar them emotionally for life.

## Keep Her Guessing

Don't reveal or make your intentions clear almost immediately. Even if you really dig a woman and tempted to tell her straight off, hold back for a while. Women love drama and an element of suspense. Mix your actions by doing both – showering her with attention as well acting aloof at times.

Just ensure you don't end up confusing her. Keep her guessing about your feelings for her. If you make her too comfortable and fuzzy, she may end up losing interest. It's all right to keep them slightly perplexed without confusing them much. If you've just begun dating someone, act totally into her one moment and nonchalant the next. This is enough to send her mind into a psychological tizzy that keeps her guessing. The sneaky little trick can keep a woman on her toes and drive her insane enough to keep her hooked!

Playing with her emotions shouldn't be misused or viewed in a negative light. If used well, it can be a perfectly workable strategy for winning your dream woman's affection and establishing a powerful emotional connection. For instance, act supportive one moment and slowly detach yourself in the next. This may appear mysterious or confusing in the beginning. However, later, she'll find herself magnetically attracted to your positive side.

## Come Across as Taken

While this is another sneaky, back-door technique, it can work wonders when it comes to drawing the woman to you like a magnet. Women are biologically wired to go after men that their competitors' desire. It sort of validates the dude's greatness when other women like him too. Women are almost always concerned about how others react to their acquisitions, which is why they need a bunch of girls in tow when they go shopping or even picking a gift for someone. Validation about their choice is important for them from an evolutionary and psychological perspective.

Thus, when someone appears like he is already taken, they tend to feel a sense of validation that the guy is indeed worthy enough of their affection. However, there may be a downside to this too. Many righteous women may prefer staying away from you if you appear taken. They don't fancy treading into someone else's territory.

# Chapter 4

# Time for an Invasion

You've now progressed to the next level and successfully established a comfort level with the woman of your dreams. There's an unmistakably warm camaraderie and a slowly building sexual chemistry. It's time to go for the kill and have roaring sex with the woman you fancy. Here are ten incredibly effective tips to get a woman sexually excited and insanely desperate to make love with you.

## Get Out of the Friend Zone

If you're like most guys, your number fear when it comes to a woman you fancy is to pray hard she doesn't friend-zone you or see you simply as a good friend. The tricky part is a majority of the time if you're friend-zoned, it is challenging for her to view you in a romantic, non-platonic manner. Here are my expert tips to avoid the dreaded friend zone.

Again, play up the competition and validation element. Give the idea you have several women desiring you, and a woman will seldom want to give or friend-zone someone whom plenty of others desire.

If you don't want to be her best friend, don't act like one. Don't play agony uncle or have innately personal conversations about her ex-partners. If she becomes too comfortable with the idea of having such personal conversations with you, she'll be running for your shoulder to cry on each time tragedy strikes, and you'll be friendzoned faster than you realize. Avoid sharing every intimate detail with her if you don't wish to be friend-zoned.

## Be a Romance King

The journey from friendship or dating to landing up in your bed can be quicker if you present a more romantic side. Of course, the idea is not to pretend being someone you're not. It's no secret that women adore men who swoon over them and sweep them off their feet with romantic gestures. Read the woman carefully to understand what she craves for, what impresses her and when you should stop.

Some women love when you flirt with them, while others are easily offended and take even harmless flirting as a sign of you wanting to go to bed with them. Don't give the impression that you are attempting to manipulate or control their feelings for sex, while also being in control of your own feelings.

Showing respect, old-fashioned chivalry and courtesy help men win a lot of brownie points with women. Notice how women have butterflies fluttering in their stomachs in the company of men who display a more gentlemanly and civilized behavior. Few things are hotter than good manners.

Women dig men who appreciate them and demonstrate the right emotion towards them. All some women want is attention, and they are quick to jump in bed with men who shower them with plenty of attention.

## Set the Stage

I'll let you in on another powerful secret to get a woman to sleep with you. The chances of a woman getting physically intimate with you is directly proportional to how much she relates to you or spends time thinking about you. Occupy a major chunk of her mindshare, and you've occupied her bed space too.

The guy who thinks about for a majority of the time is the guy she is most likely to go to bed with. Don't you want to be that dude?

One pro tip is to send her psychologically and subconsciously addictive texts. There are tons of ways to get her interested in you by sending texts to trigger psychological addiction. Ask her about her day or if she needs a little pampering. How about a relaxing body massage? A couple spa treatment probably?

Compliment her about how attractive she was looking in a particular dress she wore on the date last night. Make her feel like she's the one.

## Foreplay

Scary as it sounds, this will make or break your chances of going to bed with a woman. Don't undermine the importance of foreplay in getting a woman sexually excited. While it's relatively easy for men to be sexually drawn to an attractive woman, women are wired much differently. They don't simply fancy jumping in bed with an attractive guy, but instead they need someone they can relate to on a more emotional level.

Women love a demonstrative man who isn't afraid to reveal his fondness for them in the form of lingering touches, long smooches, and intimate hugs. Establish a close connection through these affectionate gestures before enjoying torrid sexual intercourse with her. Just because you are ready to rip apart her clothes and make love, don't assume she is.

Use these effective erotic gestures to win her before going for the kill. Cupping a woman's face is a sign of deep admiration and adoration. Start by rubbing /kissing her lower neck. Whisper sweet nothings into her ear. Kiss her lightly on her shoulder. Stare into her eyes as much as possible. Try to move slowly, smoothly and gently from neutral zones to her erogenous zones, instead of simply penetrating her.

Concentrate on the woman's erogenous zones to stimulate her yearning for sex. Try to make an effort to touch, kiss, fondle/caress and lick her in specific sensitive, intimate areas of the body. Not everyone responds to sensations/touches in the erogenous zones similarly.

Certain zones tend to be more sensitive for some women than others. The two primary erogenous regions for a woman are her feet and head. Give her a gentle foot massage or kiss her lightly on her head. Kissing during foreplay can involve licking, seductive sucking and biting. A woman's lower back, abdomen, and inner thigh region are also extremely sensitive to intimate touches. A majority of women derive great sexual pleasure from being touched in these erogenous zones.

## Create the Perfect Ambiance

When men want sex, they become pretty immune to everything around them. Women, on the other hand, are more sensitive to the environment around them. Distractions such as loud sounds, dazzling lights or even dirty bed linen can put them off from the act of sex.

Simple things like turning off the television, changing unclean bed sheets, playing soft music in the background and dimming the lights work in awakening their sexual desire. Make the place aglow with soft candlelight (preferably nice smelling aroma candles), since low light and scent both can act as active triggers for lighting a woman's sexual desires. Use bright furnishings in the bedroom.

Candles not just create an exciting and intimate mood but also go a long way in making the woman feel less insecurity (especially if you haven't gone to bed with her before) about getting undressed or revealing her body.

Colors such as red, orange, purple, etc. convey passion, energy, enthusiasm, and strength. Bright red linen or curtains can wonder the bedroom. These are all stimuli that act at a subconscious level to stimulate a woman's deep-seated desires. It talks to the woman at a very subconscious level that you care to put in a lot of effort to get her excited about the prospect of having sex with you.

Music is an important part of the set-up. It needs to resonate with the night's seductive and sexy theme, however, don't make it too loud or distracting. Concentrate on your togetherness than playing a personal favorite playlist. Dude, you may dig death metal but doesn't appeal to a majority of women. Some types of music can accentuate the romance or intimacy, but most are a huge distraction or turn-off for women. Ask her what type of music she prefers to score big with her.

## Brush Up Your Kissing Skills

Kissing is a huge turn on for both men and women. There are volumes of books dedicated to the fine art of kissing because that is indeed the stairway to get a woman excited about going to bed with you. If you get this right, the woman will be yearning to go to bed with you. Too often, men are close to sleeping with a woman they desire and ruin it with their awkward kissing skills, which is a big turn off.

Start by holding a woman close to you. Linger on with the gaze for a few seconds longer than usual. Look straight into her eyes, and speak to them. Brush your lips lightly against hers for a few seconds and pull back. Do this a few times teasingly, before holding her lips with yours. Slowly, bring in your tongue, and place the tip of the tongue on her lips. Don't start drooling or indulge in sucking her lips. This is all the more important if it's your first kiss as a couple.

Keep your breath awesome. Bad breath is a huge turn-off. If you have even a slight inkling of stinky breath, chew some mint or gum to keep the foul breath at bay before going on a date. A golden kissing rule – always keep your eyes open while kissing. It strengthens the connection subconsciously and gets your girl even more excited.

Always leave the lady wanting more when it comes to kissing. You'll get clues to her kissing style in the way she responds to your kissing overtures. How does the woman kiss you back? If you're perceptive enough, you'll get a good idea about what she truly enjoys. Just keeping doing more of what she's leading you to do.

## Build Sexual Tension

At times, a woman will be extremely horny and ready for roaring sex without you having to try too hard. Yet, you need to work towards building sexual tension in the beginning.

What exactly is this sexual tension that is referred to throughout the book? Sexual tension is nothing but an exciting feeling occurring between two people who feel a compelling physical attraction for each other, however physical intimacy is delayed owing to their unique circumstances, environment, personality, etc.

For instance, even though a woman is strongly attracted to you sexually, she may not want to come across as too easy to get laid. Similarly, two people may be working together in an organization that doesn't really encourage personal relationships between co-workers. Sometimes, either of the partners may already be committed to someone else, which may not go beyond foreplay or making out.

Building sexual tension by delaying gratification is a great way to keep the woman begging for sex. Women really dig the exciting feeling of releasing the sexual tension built up over a period of time. They love the idea of building up tension through kissing, making out and touching each other. Don't undermine the importance of creating sexual tension when it comes to enjoying torrid sexual encounters.

You can enjoy a few brief and exciting make-out sessions before finally taking her to bed after building plenty of sexual tension. You may want to send a host of pre-sex texts that establish that you are attracted enough to want her in bed.

Avoid telling the woman straight off that you want to sleep with her. It may just ruin the excitement you've been trying to create over a period of time. Allow her to feel a strong connection with you before she decides to take it to another level. Play it gently and slowly, warm up before going full throttle in bed and ensure she's in the right mood to get intimate with you.

Having a slightly dirty conversation is also a good way to build sexual chemistry. How do you start? Simple. Pose a question that appears innocent but paves the way for something crazily dirty. Before you both even realize, you will be pinning for each other.

Some men like to set the pace for excitement by indulging in phone sex before going for real sex. It's a great way to understand your girl's sexual fantasies and appetite for sex! Watch out for the verbal clues she offers while talking about sexual acts.

## Don't Make Sex Your Only Intention

Don't make sex your only intention with the woman you desire. If you seem too pushy or easy, it won't be a challenging prospect for them to go to bed with you. The secret sauce is to be the exact opposite of what most are (yearning for sex). A majority of men are simply operating with the intention of getting a woman to go to bed with them. When your approach is different, you stand out.

You move away from the desperate trap to act more in control of getting the woman to do what you want. Don't try to persuade her to sleep with you. Rather make her feel like she should convince you to go to bed with her. Chances are women make up their minds pretty quickly about guys they want to get intimate with. Even before you can think "sexy boobs" to yourself, she knows whether she wants to share them with you.

Women are used to guys drooling over them. If you make it a challenging prospect for them to go to bed with you by acting like you're not very keen on sleeping with them, it'll make the prospect even more exciting for them. Do something that women are not accustomed to, and you'll have them eating out of your hands. Don't make yourself an easy conquest.

Demonstrate through your actions that you're not going to be an effortless acquisition and that she has to work really hard to get you. This makes the proposition of wooing you even more exciting for the woman.

## Understand Her Fantasies

Don't make sex a cut and dry chore or mechanical task for your dream woman once she looks ready to go to bed with you. Before you take her to bed, try to understand her fantasies. Avoid freaking out if it includes Brad Pitt.

Instead, make it work to your advantage. Role-playing and fulfilling fantasies are one of the best ways to get women hooked and keep the sexual spice intact. Things won't go stale if you are creating various exciting and stimulating sexual situations in the sack.

One amazing tip for triggering a woman's sexual fantasies is to initiate things or get things to spice up in the most unexpected places. Of course, no one's asking you to get into trouble with the authorities, but a little frisky behavior goes a long way in getting someone to feel a compelling urge to go to bed with you.

It is easy for dating couples to do the expected or slip into a routine/standard cycle (meeting, dating, hooking up, getting hitched, etc.). Try to approach her for making our or hooking up in a totally unexpected place.

Identifying and meeting a woman's need is the best bed to keep her hooked to you in bed. When you go to purchase a car, does the smooth-talking salesman simply flash a sports car and inquire if you liked it enough to buy it? No right?

He'll first inquire if you want a car that gives great mileage or one that accelerates fast or one that gives you a good control while driving through rougher roads. Later, he'll match it with your requirement, and you'll be like "wonderful, this is precisely what I wanted." Learn to personify what others seek in you. If the woman you're with seeks a lot of adventure, excitement, and independence, do your darnedest best to give her exactly that.

## Display Patience

Nowadays every girl is wary of being used for sex and then dumped like a hot potato for the next hottest thing. It is easy for them to assume based on past experiences that all you want to do is go to bed with them. These negative thoughts playing in their mind may make your charm appear more manipulative and fake, even if you genuinely care about her.

Try not to come across as aggressive, pushy or affected when things go according to how you desire. Be prepared for unexpected things. Stay calm, gentle and sweet even in the face of rejection. Once the woman sees you as someone who has the ability to be nice despite not having his way, she's likelier to get rid of the defense walls built around her. It may simply be her way of testing your patience or how serious you are about trying to make an effort to win her affection. Women can play a lot of hard to get games to try your patience. If you tide through these tactics confidently and patiently, you'll win her respect.

Historically, psychologically and evolutionarily, physical intimacy is a big deal for women. They treat it with probably the same measure of seriousness that you would treat say purchasing a new car or signing up for a new home. They don' just sign on the physical intimacy papers without you giving them a compelling reason to do so. And you know only too well once a car buyer walks away from making a purchase, he almost never returns. It is the same with women.

Display patience when it comes to understanding the woman's ideas and values related to physical intimacy.

# Chapter 5

# The Evil Within You, You Can be Her Poison

Well, so now that you've slowly established your intention to take her to bed or even slept with her, how do you get her hooked to you or earn her unwavering loyalty, so she doesn't look elsewhere. I've got your back here too. Here are some of the best tips to get your woman addicted to you.

## Introduce Her to Your Friends

A great way to get a woman hooked to you is by introducing her and including her in your gang of buddies. This is your way of showing her you value her enough to be included in your inner coterie.

Be warm and affectionate with her in the company of your friends. Allow her to feel a sense of belongingness with the group.

Compliment her about something that's unique to her. She'll be floored on being showered with affection and respect publically and will reciprocate by keeping you happy and staying loyal to you.

## Use the Power of Words

Women are high on words, verbal creatures. Why do you think they listen so intently to soulful lyrics of musicians such as Tracy Chapman and Phil Collins? Their words are rich with emotions that tug at your heartstrings. Words are a deep way of connecting with people because they awaken certain sensations inside you.

Write old-fashioned and intimate love letters to your woman. Move your woman with the right words. If you master the art of using the perfect words at the perfect time, you'll get to bed and keep them there faster than you can imagine. Just ensure to keep it genuine, so it doesn't sound contrived or falsely flattering.

## Pamper Her

This one's no secret sauce yet it's baffling how many guys never get it. Women love to be pampered and showered with undivided attention. Cook a simple yet delicious meal for her (bonus points if it's her favorite food). Play soft music in the background. Decorate the room with colorful flowers.

Keep a bottle of her favorite wine ready. Make it a memorable evening by enjoying a stimulating conversation. Be a smooth talker, as well as infuse your conversation with plenty of humor and compliments. The wine will get you both to feel giddy-headed and get things heated up in bed. Pamper her with unexpected gestures, and she'll be floored enough to be completely hooked to you.

## Be Suave and Valuable

It doesn't hurt to be fashionable or dress nattily to remain desirable in the eyes of your woman. Make a constant effort to be more polished, suave and romantic. Always yourself more valuable, and act like you know your true worth.  We know by now that women crave the attention of alpha males with high self-value who are desired by many

It's the world's worst kept secret that women are fundamentally driven by their emotions and not by logic. Don't make the mistake of trying to use rationale with a woman to influence or persuade her. Instead, appeal to her emotions by focusing on romance, affection, and demonstrations of love.

## Tell Her You Are Thinking About Her

Most men never understand the importance of letting a woman know that they are thinking about her. Show a woman how she's on your mind 24 by 7, and you'll have her positively enslaved. To retain her affection, you have to show that you think about her even when she's not physically there with you. This one tip will have her swooning over you and more often than not attract her loyalty.

Women are innately emotional creatures who crave attention and security. They are subconsciously highly territorial in nature when it comes to relationships, they can even intuitively identify certain signs that indicate the relationship is under threat. Don't ignore her calls and messages, which send a feeling of being emotionally distanced. This doesn't mean you drop her a message every 5 seconds. Sending simple yet thoughtful messages (inquiring about her day or telling her how you kiss her home-cooked meals or reminding her to take her medicines) throughout the day can go a long way in keeping the connection alive.

# Game is On!

- 64 -

I thank you for making it through to the very end of *Attract Women*.

I genuinely hope you enjoyed reading it. I also hope the book has armed you with a host of actionable, practical and result-oriented strategies to not just attract/control women through body language and mind controlling techniques but also keep them hooked to you.

The next step is to simply use all proven secrets described in the book and transform your dating and sex life. Apply these little-known yet highly effective tips to be the ultimate woman magnet or alpha male. Now that you know how women think and feel use these psychological tricks to earn their complete love, respect, and loyalty. Get them to obey you and do exactly what you want by implementing these easy to use everyday techniques.

Be a confident, charming, enjoyable and irresistible woman magnet!

I will see you in the playground!

## Leave a Review

- 65 -

# Thank you for reading, hope you can leave a few kind words.

*Your review will motivate us to do better.*

*I will see you in the playground!*

**VICTORIA LYNX**

*Blue Labyrinth Pte Ltd, 2019*

# All Our Books

- 66 -

*Follow me to stay up-to-date with my new books!*